ACCOUNTING LIFEPAC 1
ACCOUNTING OVERVIEW

M000311506

OVERVIEW

An understanding of bookkeeping and accounting is essential to anyone interested in a business career. This understanding is necessary because of the importance of accurate recording and reporting of business transactions. We should understand the basic principles of bookkeeping in order to maintain our own personal financial records. These records are important so that we are able to manage our finances to satisfy our basic needs and wants.

OBJECTIVES

When you have completed this LIFEPAC, you will be able to:

1. Understand the nature of accounting.
2. Identify accounting concepts.
3. Define a proprietorship, partnership and corporation.
4. List the advantages and disadvantages of a proprietorship, partnership, and corporation.
5. Define accounting terms related to the accounting equation.
6. Identify the components of the accounting equation.
7. Classify accounts as assets, liabilities, or owner's equity.
8. Make changes in the accounting equation and explain the effect on each element of that equation.
9. Analyze how these changes affect the accounts in the accounting equation.
10. Prove the equality of assets, liabilities and capital from the information provided by the basic accounting equation after each transaction.

VOCABULARY

Accountant – a person responsible for interpreting financial data.

Asset – anything of value that is owned.

Basic accounting equation – a formula that illustrates the relationship between assets, liabilities and capital.

Bookkeeper – a person responsible for recording business transactions.

Business entity – the existence of a business as an artificial individual.

Business transaction – business activity that causes changes in the value of assets, liabilities and capital.

Capital – the financial interest of the owner of a business; determined by subtracting total liabilities from the total assets. Also called Owner's Equity.

Corporation – an association of individuals united for a common purpose to use a common name and to change members without dissolving the association; a business chartered under state law and owned by stockholders.

Drawing – an owner's withdrawal of cash from his business for personal use.

Equities – the claims against the assets of a business.

Fiscal period – the period of time that the books are open to record transactions and summarize accounting information.

Liability – any amount that is owed.

Partnership – an association of two or more persons to carry on as co-owners of a business for profit.

Proprietor – the owner of a business.

Revenue – the increase in owner's equity caused by income from the sale of goods and services.

Sole proprietorship – a business owned and managed by one person.

Grace

ACCOUNTING LIFEPAC® 1
ACCOUNTING OVERVIEW

CONTENTS

Author: **Daniel L. Ritzman, B.S.**

Editors: Alan Christopherson, M.S.

                        Jennifer L. Davis, B.S.

Alpha Omega Publications®

804 N. 2nd Ave. E., Rock Rapids, IA 51246-1759

© MM by Alpha Omega Publications, Inc.   All rights reserved.

LIFEPAC is a registered trademark of Alpha Omega Publications, Inc.

LIFEPAC®

Accounting
Student Book

Unit **1**

SECTION I. THE NATURE OF BOOKKEEPING & ACCOUNTING

Career Opportunities

The nature of accounting is to provide accurate financial information needed by a business to succeed in a competitive business environment. This information is needed by owners, managers, creditors and government agencies.

The **bookkeeper** is the person responsible for *recording* business transactions, while the **accountant** has the responsibility of *interpreting* that data. The data is compiled in the necessary reports to help management make sound business decisions that include:

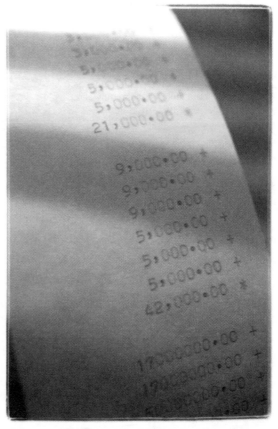

1. Determining the price of goods or services provided by the business;

2. Determining the profit or loss from production of goods or providing a service;

3. Determining the cost of and profit from adding new goods or services;

4. Determining how to cut costs without affecting quality or service;

5. Determining how much to borrow;

6. Determining if a loan can be obtained;

7. Determining state and federal income taxes;

8. Determining the legality of a business operation; and

9. Determining if governmental regulations are being followed.

Many career opportunities exist for a person to provide these essential business services. The job availability covers the entire financial community which includes business, government and nonprofit organizations (churches, YMCA, etc). The choice of a career is entirely up to you. Listed below are some of the career choices you have in the accounting field.

General Office Clerk

Job Responsibilities: General office tasks including bookkeeping, word processing and secretarial duties.

Education: High school diploma with at least one year of accounting and computer applications.

OFFICE WORK. PT. Good w/figures. Flexible hours.

Clerks Wanted Exc. Hrs., Exc. Salary. For Appt. call 555-1234

RECEPTIONIST/Bookkeeper Duties incl acct pay, data entry, inventory control. FT. Comp salary & benefits. eoe

---

Accounting Clerk

Job Responsibilities: Record, sort and file accounting information.

Types of Clerks: Payroll Clerk, Accounts Payable Clerk, Accounts Receivable Clerk, Receiving Clerk, etc.

Education: High school diploma with a minimum of one year of accounting and computer applications. Recommend a two-year program.

> **ACCOUNTS RECEIVABLE:**
> P/T. temp position, for 6-8 wks in Binghamton area. Must possess good data entry & computer skills. Medicare billing, exp. preferred

> **ACCOUNTS RECEIVABLE CLERK - PT**
> 12-5 pm Long-term to perm.

> **Payroll Specialist.** Exp. in payroll data entry & payroll tax

> **Accounts Payable/Clerical**
> Immediate opening. Reqs. strong organizational, communication & detail skills. Exp. preparing invoices, data entry, filing & general office. Microsoft Word & Excel knowledge. FT. Send resume & career objective letter to:

Bookkeeper

Job Responsibilities: General accounting which includes recording and summarizing accounting information.

Education: High school diploma with a minimum of two years of accounting and at least one year of computer applications. Many employers strongly suggest additional education in accounting, either in a community college or business school.

> **Accounting Paraprofessional**
> PT flex hrs. exp. w/computer, bookkeeping, payroll & sales tax; prep of personal/corp. tax returns.

> **ACCOUNTANT**
> CPA firm seeking CPA or candidate. 2+ years public experience preferred.

Accountant

Job Responsibilities: Summarize, analyze and interpret accounting information.

Types of Accounting: Tax, governmental, managerial, financial and non-profit organizations.

Education: High school diploma with a major in accounting plus additional education in a community college or business school. A two- to four-year program is recommended.

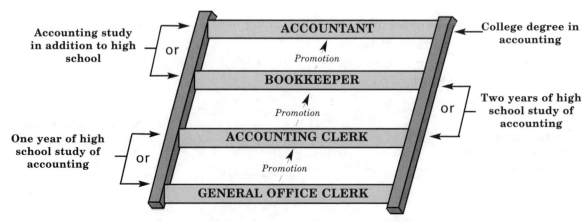

4

Accounting Concepts and Terms

The accounting profession is guided by basic accounting concepts. These concepts are applied when designing a financial system, interpreting accounting records and creating business reports. All accounting concepts will be applied as we continue our study of bookkeeping and accounting.

Business Entity: A business is considered an entity (an individual). Therefore, all business financial information is entered and reported separately from the owner's personal financial records. It is very important that the business owner have very defined accounting systems to keep personal and business information completely segregated.

Accounting Period Cycle: Changes in the financial information are prepared for a specific period of time. This period of time can be a month, a quarter, semi-annually, or annually. Many businesses use an annual reporting cycle to aid in the preparation of tax reports. This cycle is known as a **fiscal period**.

Objective Evidence: Every business transaction is supported by a source document to prove the transaction occurred.

Unit of Measurement: All transactions are recorded in a unit of measurement such as the dollar.

Realization of Revenue: Income from a business transaction is recorded and accounted for at the time goods or services are sold.

Matching Expenses with Revenue: All revenue and expenses associated with a business activity are recorded in the same accounting period.

Historical Costs: The actual amount of money paid or received is the amount actually entered in the accounting records.

Adequate Disclosure: All financial statements should contain all information needed for any person to understand the business's financial condition.

Consistent Reporting: The same accounting concepts are applied the same way for each accounting period for as long as the business operates.

Review the material in this section in preparation for the Self Test. The Self Test will check your mastery of this particular section. The items missed on this Self Test will indicate specific areas where restudy is needed for mastery.

SELF TEST 1

Match the following accounting concepts with their definitions (each answer, 5 points).

1.01 ___g___ a specific period of time during which business transactions are recorded

1.02 ___d___ a business is considered an individual

1.03 ___e___ every business transaction is supported by a source document

1.04 ___c___ the same accounting concepts are applied the same way for each accounting period

1.05 ___h___ the dollar, for example

1.06 ___f___ the actual amount of money paid or received is the amount that is entered into the accounting records

1.07 ___b___ all financial statements should contain the information necessary to understand the financial condition of the business

1.08 ___i___ income from transactions is recorded at the time goods or services are sold

1.09 ___a___ all revenue and expenses associated with a business activity are recorded in the same accounting period

a. Matching Expenses with Revenue

b. Adequate Disclosure

c. Consistent Reporting

d. Business Entity

e. Objective Evidence

f. Historical Costs

g. Accounting Period Cycle

h. Unit of Measurement

i. Realization of Revenue

Complete these activities (each answer, 5 points).

1.010 Describe the difference between a bookkeeper and an accountant _A Bookkeeper records and summarizes accounting information, an Accountant summarizes, analyzes & interprets it._

1.011 List three career opportunities that are available in the accounting field:

a. _Bookkeeper_

b. _Accounting Clerk_

c. _Accountant_

Score _____

Adult Check _____

Initial   Date

SECTION II. THE FORMATION OF A BUSINESS

An important element of America's free enterprise system is that nearly all businesses are owned and operated by individuals. A person (or a group of people) invest in a business with the hope of making a profit from the business activity.

Types of Business Ownership

Business ownership may take different legal forms—each has its own privileges and responsibilities. The three most common forms of business ownership are:

1. **The sole proprietorship:** An individual owns the business, assumes all risks and operates based on his/her own personal goals.

2. **The partnership:** As defined by the Uniform Partnership Act, a partnership "...is an association of two or more persons to carry on as co-owners of a business for profit."

3. **The corporation:** Defined by the United States Supreme Court as "...an association of individuals united for some common purpose and permitted by law to use a common name and to change its members without dissolution of the association."

The form of ownership depends on the following factors:

1. Capital (startup and working capital);
2. Legal status;
3. Transferability of ownership;
4. Owner's liability for debts;
5. Ease of organization;
6. Ease of dissolution;
7. Governmental regulations; and
8. Continuity of ownership.

The **sole proprietorship** is the most common form of business ownership in the United States. This form of ownership is especially suited for a small business, particularly those just beginning. A sole proprietorship is a business owned and managed by one person. The owner is known as the **proprietor**.

The sole proprietorship is commonly referred to as a "common law" form of business organization because there are no federal, state, or local regulations to govern the startup or termination of legal operations. Since the startup process is relatively easy, we find that sole proprietorships make up about 70% of the total businesses in the United States but only produce 15% of the total dollar volume of all business transactions.

The following charts show a comparison of the advantages and disadvantages of these three common types of business ownership: a sole proprietorship, a partnership and a corporation.

SOLE PROPRIETORSHIP

ADVANTAGES	DISADVANTAGES
1. **Ownership of All Profits:** The owner is entitled to 100% of the profits earned.	1. **Unlimited Liability:** The owner's assets maybe used to satisfy any creditors' claims. If the business assets do not cancel all debt, the owner's personal property may be used to satisfy all claims.
2. **Owner is Boss:** Being your own boss is probably the most important concept of a sole proprietorship.	2. **Limited Financial Resources:** The owner's ability to borrow depends largely on his/her own resources. Some banks and other creditors are hesitant to lend money or extend credit to single proprietorships because of what they feel to be a higher risk factor.
3. **Decision Making:** The owner's decisions are final. This concept speeds up the decision-making process, thus allowing the owner to make timely business decisions that can result in better profits and sometimes a step up on the competition.	3. **Management Problems:** Owners must apply their own skills to management. They assume all managerial tasks. Many fail because of the lack of management skills.
4. **Tax Savings:** No special taxes are levied against a sole proprietorship. The owner is only responsible for federal and state income taxes as well as all normal business taxes such as payroll taxes, etc.	4. **Lack of Continuity:** Death, insanity, imprisonment, bankruptcy, or retirement of the owner of a sole proprietorship will terminate the business.
5. **Secrecy:** There are no legal requirements to make public any financial statements as to the condition of the business, nor any other confidential information. This provides a competitive advantage for the proprietor.	
6. **Ease of Organization and Dissolution:** A sole proprietorship has very few legal complications to get started. Dissolution is accomplished quickly because no legal procedures are needed.	

PARTNERSHIP

ADVANTAGES	DISADVANTAGES
1. **Ease of Organization:** A partnership agreement is drawn up to tell how much money each partner will contribute, what responsibilities each will have and how the profits (and losses) will be divided.	1. **Unlimited Liability:** Each partner's assets maybe used to satisfy any creditors' claims. If the business assets do not cancel all debt, the personal property of the partners may be used to satisfy all claims. An individual partner may also be held financially responsible for the debts of the business if the other partners cannot pay their share.
2. **Shared Responsibility:** The success or failure of the business does not depend solely on the efforts of one individual.	2. **Limited Financial Resources:** Even with two or more partners, the capital in a venture of this type is limited to what monies the partners are able to raise on their own.
3. **Talents and Resources are Pooled:** Each partner brings certain skills and abilities to the business and decisions are made jointly.	3. **Management Problems:** Since the authority to operate the business is divided, disagreements between partners can sometimes create problems.
4. **Shared Financial Resources:** The initial investment in a partnership is usually greater than a sole proprietorship because the financial resources of two or more people are available.	4. **Lack of Continuity:** The partnership is legally terminated with the death or withdrawal of one of the partners or if a new partner is added.
5. **Better Credit Rating:** Credit may be easier to obtain because the responsibility of the debt is upon more than just a single individual. If one partner defaults on a debt, the other partner becomes responsible.	

CORPORATION

ADVANTAGES	DISADVANTAGES
1. **Limited Liability:** Stockholders are not personally liable for the debts of a corporation. The losses of stockholders are limited to the amount each individual has invested and their personal property cannot be taken to satisfy any corporate obligations.	1. **Greater Tax Liability:** A corporation must pay income tax on its profits. In addition, the part of the profits that is distributed to the shareholders as a dividend is also subject to income tax, since the shareholders must declare the dividend as part of their income.
2. **Longevity:** The corporation remains intact regardless of changes in stock ownership or changes in management. The corporation has continuous life.	2. **Greater Regulation:** There are many laws and regulations, some of them quite restrictive, that are placed upon corporations by state and federal governments.
3. **Ownership Easily Transferred:** The stock certificates held by each stockholder act as proof of ownership and can be easily and legally transferred from one individual to another.	3. **Complicated and Costly Organization:** A corporation is much more costly and complicated to start than a partnership or single proprietorship, due in part to the number of laws and regulations that govern their operation.
4. **Better Management:** The officers of corporations are usually experienced professional managers.	
5. **Increased Investment:** Since they are financed by the sale of stock, corporations can raise large amounts of money by selling shares of their stock.	

Review the material in this section in preparation for the following Self Test. This Self Test will check your mastery of this particular section as well as your knowledge of the previous section.

SELF TEST 2

List five factors that determine what form of ownership a business will have (each answer, 5 points).

2.01
a. Capitol (startup and working capitol)
b. Legal status
c. Ease of organization
d. Governmental regulations
e. Continuity of ownership

Identify the following descriptions by writing S **for a sole proprietorship,** P **for a partnership or** C **for a corporation** (each answer, 3 points).

2.02	P	owned by two or more persons who are co-owners
2.03	P	talents and resources are pooled
2.04	S	owned by one individual
2.05	C	a "common law" form of business organization
2.06	C	has a much greater tax liability
2.07	P	credit may be easier to obtain because of shared responsibility
2.08	S	owner is entitled to 100% of profits earned
2.09	C	usually managed by experienced professionals
2.010	C	financed by sale of shares of stock
2.011	S	easiest to organize and/or dissolve
2.012	S	no legal requirements to make any public financial statements
2.013	S	owner has unlimited liability
2.014	S	the most common form of business ownership in the United States
2.015	C	can change its members without dissolution of the association
2.016	P	disagreements about management can sometimes create problems
2.017	P	produces only 15% of the total dollar volume of all business transactions
2.018	C	ownership is easily transferred without dissolving the organization
2.019	C	subject to many state and federal regulations
2.020	S	very complicated and costly to start
2.021	P	initial investment is greater because of shared financial resources

68 / 85

Score _____

Adult Check _____
           Initial   Date

11

SECTION III. THE ACCOUNTING SYSTEM

Elements of Accounting

Proprietors and managers need accurate financial records in order to properly manage a business and prepare the required reports. The type of business and the size of a business usually determines how accounting records are kept. These records can be produced by manual methods, by accounting machines, or by computers. However, the method chosen does not change the accounting concepts and principles that are applied.

A business operates with items such as cash, inventories, supplies, accounts receivables and insurance. These items a business owns or controls are called **assets**. Therefore, an asset is anything of value owned or controlled by a business entity. Ownership of the assets is not required. Under certain circumstances, *control* of an item is enough to list it as an asset. For example, a machine that is leased could be listed as a business asset because it is controlled by the entity and the entity receives the benefits from its use. Claims against those assets are called **equities**. These claims against business assets are divided between the owner and the institutions to whom a business owes money.

Since there are two classifications of claims against the business assets, it is important to maintain records that clearly divide the business financial records from any person or other entity that may have an equity in that business.

The two equity classifications are:

1. **Equities of a person or business to whom the entity owes money**. Any amount owed is called a **liability**.
2. **Equities of the owner.** The owner's equity is called **capital**. It is important to stress at this point that the owner's equity is the remaining value of all assets after all debts (liabilities) are paid.

The Basic Accounting Equation

Accountants have developed an equation to illustrate the relationship between assets, liabilities and capital. This equation is called the **Basic Accounting Equation**. The equation reflects the equality of assets on the one side with the claims of the creditors and the equity of the owner on the other side. This means that a business possesses assets subject to the rights of its creditors and owner.

The Basic Accounting Equation: ASSETS = LIABILITIES + CAPITAL

The accounting equation must always balance. Therefore, the left side (the assets side) must equal the total of the right side (liabilities plus capital). Like any mathematical equation, the basic accounting equation can be changed to reflect different approaches to keep the books in balance.

The original form, **A = L + C**, focuses on the *assets* of the entity. However, it can be changed to stress the owner's *capital* as follows: **C = A − L.**

Another arrangement illustrates the creditors' equity or *liabilities* as follows: **L = A − C.**

By using the proper form of the basic accounting equation, the dollar value of any part can easily be calculated if the dollar value of the other two parts are known.

 Complete the following activities.

3.1   A business has $50 in liabilities and $80 in capital. Calculate the value of the *assets*.

$$
\begin{aligned}
\textit{Assets} \quad &= \quad \textit{Liabilities} \ + \ \textit{Capital} \\
A \quad &= \quad L \ + \ C \\
A \quad &= \quad \$50 \ + \ \$80 \\
A \quad &= \quad \underline{\hspace{2cm}}
\end{aligned}
$$

3.2   A business has assets worth $180 and liabilities of $60. Calculate the value of the owner's equity (*capital*).

$$
\begin{aligned}
\textit{Capital} \quad &= \quad \textit{Assets} \ - \ \textit{Liabilities} \\
C \quad &= \quad A \ - \ L \\
C \quad &= \quad \$180 \ - \ \$60 \\
C \quad &= \quad \underline{\hspace{2cm}}
\end{aligned}
$$

3.3   A business has assets with a value of $220 and capital (*owner's equity*) of $150. Calculate the equity of the creditors (*liabilities*).

$$
\begin{aligned}
\textit{Liabilities} \quad &= \quad \textit{Assets} \ - \ \textit{Capital} \\
L \quad &= \quad A \ - \ C \\
L \quad &= \quad \$220 \ - \ \$150 \\
L \quad &= \quad \underline{\hspace{2cm}}
\end{aligned}
$$

Determine the missing amount in each of the accounting equations below.

	Assets	=	*Liabilities*	+	*Capital*
3.4	$8,000	=	$2,000	+	_____
3.5	_____	=	$3,200	+	$2,800
3.6	$2,500	=	_____	+	$1,900
3.7	_____	=	$1,800	+	$1,800

13

How Transactions Affect the Accounting Equation

Every business will be continually changing the value of assets, liabilities and capital. These changes are brought about by **business transactions**. Although each item in the equation will change as the business operates, the elements must still remain in balance.

The changes caused by business transactions can be grouped as follows:

CHANGES TO OWNER'S EQUITY

Increases: Investments of additional capital.

Revenue earned from the sale of goods or services.

Decreases: Withdrawals of cash from the business for personal use (**drawing**).

Expenses resulting from the operation of the business in the process of earning revenue.

Incurring a debt (liability) on behalf of the business. The debt can be incurred from borrowing funds to operate or by purchasing merchandise for resale on credit.

CHANGES TO ASSETS

Increases: Cash received from the exchange of goods or services.

Value of goods or services sold on account to charge customers.

Assets gained from a bank loan or loan from another business entity.

Decreases: Cash paid for the daily expenses incurred to produce revenue.

Cash paid to settle debts.

Cash paid to the owner as a withdrawal for personal use.

There are business transactions that will *not* change the total assets value of the equation. You may think of it as trading assets; that is, using one asset (cash) to buy another asset such as supplies, equipment, or insurance.

Also to be considered are business transactions that have an effect on the owner's equity (capital). One example is trading business assets. Using the value of one asset to purchase another will *not* change the owner's equity; for example, paying cash for supplies.

The second item is buying an asset on account. For example, the owner purchases a business automobile on the installment plan.

The third situation is paying the monthly installment for the business asset purchased on account.

Accounting Concepts to Remember

1. Every business transaction changes at least two accounts in the accounting equation.
2. If the changes occur only on one side of the equation, all increases on that side must be matched with decreases on the same side.
3. If the transaction increases one side of the equation, then the other side must be increased by the same amount.
4. If the transaction decreases one side of the equation, then the other side must be decreased by the same amount.

Recording Business Transactions

It is the job of the bookkeeper to record business transactions in a meaningful process, balancing them one by one with the accounting equation.

Business Transactions of Joe Jones, Accountant:

1. Owner invested $6,000 cash to begin his practice.
2. Bought supplies for $500 cash.
3. Bought office equipment on account from Office Max, $2,000.
4. Received $3,500 in accounting fees during the month.
5. Paid office rent for the month, $700.
6. Paid salaries for the month, $1,200.
7. Paid Office Max $1,200 on account.
8. Paid Mang Association $700 for insurance.
9. Withdrew $600 for personal use.

To analyze a transaction, the following must be considered:

- What accounts are affected?
- What is each account classification? (Asset, Liability, or Capital)
- How is the balance affected? (Increase or Decrease)

The business transactions of Joe Jones, Accountant are analyzed on the following pages.

15

Transaction: Owner invested $6,000 cash to begin his practice.

Mr. Jones invested cash in his new business. This transaction opened an asset account (Cash) and created the owner's equity (Capital).

Transaction	Accounts Affected	Account Classification	Change in Balance
1. Owner invested $6,000 cash to begin his practice.	Cash	Asset	Increase
	Capital	Capital	Increase

ASSETS = LIABILITIES + CAPITAL

TRANS NO.	CASH	SUPPLIES	EQUIPMENT	ACCOUNTS PAYABLE	CAPITAL
1.	+ 6,000				6,000
		PROOF	6,000 =	PROOF	6,000

Summary: The business received money; therefore, the asset Cash increased. The owner was the source for the revenue, thus causing Joe Jones, Capital to increase. After the transactions, note that the accounting equation is still in balance (left and right are equal).

Transaction: Purchased supplies for $500 cash.

Mr. Jones bought supplies (copier paper, accounting pads and adding machine tape) creating a new asset, Supplies. He used cash for payment. Actually, Mr. Jones traded the value of one asset (Cash) for the value of another (Supplies).

Transaction	Accounts Affected	Account Classification	Change in Balance
2. Purchased supplies for $500 cash.	Supplies	Asset	Increase
	Cash	Asset	Decrease

ASSETS = LIABILITIES + CAPITAL

TRANS NO.	CASH	SUPPLIES	EQUIPMENT	ACCOUNTS PAYABLE	CAPITAL
	+ 6,000				6,000
2.	− 500	+ 500			
	5,500	500			6,000
		PROOF	6,000 =	PROOF	6,000

Summary: The cash balance of the business decreased because it paid money to purchase supplies. With this purchase, the asset account Supplies increased. The owner's equity remained unchanged. However, the accounting equation is still in balance.

Transaction: Purchased office equipment on account from Office Max, $2,000.

Since the purchase was made on account, it created a business liability. Mr. Jones also has a new asset called Equipment.

Transaction	Accounts Affected	Account Classification	Change in Balance
3. Purchased office equipment on account from Office Max, $2,000.	Equipment	Asset	Increase
	Accounts Payable	Liability	Increase

ASSETS   = LIABILITIES + CAPITAL

TRANS NO.	CASH	SUPPLIES	EQUIPMENT	ACCOUNTS PAYABLE	CAPITAL
	5,500	500			6,000
3.			2,000	2,000	
	5,500	500	2,000	2,000	6,000
	PROOF		8,000	= PROOF	8,000

Summary: The business assets increased by the purchase of equipment. The new asset is called Equipment. Since the business set payment for a future date (buying on account), it created a liability called Accounts Payable. Note the accounting equation is still in balance.

~~~~~~

Transaction: Received $3,500 in accounting fees during the month.

Mr. Jones received cash for services rendered. He has more cash in the bank following this transaction. His equity is also changed because he produced the revenue.

Transaction	Accounts Affected	Account Classification	Change in Balance
4. Received $3,500 accounting fees during the month.	Cash	Asset	Increase
	Capital	Capital	Increase

<center>ASSETS   = LIABILITIES + CAPITAL</center>

TRANS NO.	CASH	SUPPLIES	EQUIPMENT	ACCOUNTS PAYABLE	CAPITAL
	5,500	500	2,000	2,000	6,000
4.	+3,500				+3,500
	9,000	500	2,000	2,000	9,500
	PROOF		11,500	= PROOF	11,500

Summary: The business received cash and thus increased its value. Determining the reason for the increase was next. The revenue was incurred by performing a business service. All revenues are transferred to the owner as an increase in equity.

<center>17</center>

Transaction: Paid office rent for the month, $700.

Mr. Jones has less cash in the bank following this transaction. His equity is also affected because he paid a business operating expense.

Transaction	Accounts Affected	Account Classification	Change in Balance
5. Paid office rent for the month, $700.	Capital	Capital	Decrease
	Cash	Asset	Decrease

	ASSETS			= LIABILITIES + CAPITAL	
TRANS NO.	CASH	SUPPLIES	EQUIPMENT	ACCOUNTS PAYABLE	CAPITAL
	9,000	500	2,000	2,000	9,500
5.	−700				−700
	8,300	500	2,000	2,000	8,800
	PROOF	10,800	=	PROOF	10,800

Summary: Anytime a business pays out cash, the cash value decreases. This cash was used to pay for a business operating expense. Since the owner's equity reflects revenue earned by operations (an increase), the owner's equity must also reflect the expenses of operations (a decrease). As illustrated, the Cash account decreased and the owner's Capital also decreased. The accounting equation is still in balance.

Transaction: Paid salaries for the month, $1,200.

Mr. Jones has less cash in the bank following this transaction. His equity is also affected because he paid a business operating expense.

Transaction	Accounts Affected	Account Classification	Change in Balance
6. Paid salaries for the month, $1,200.	Capital	Capital	Decrease
	Cash	Asset	Decrease

	ASSETS			= LIABILITIES + CAPITAL	
TRANS NO.	CASH	SUPPLIES	EQUIPMENT	ACCOUNTS PAYABLE	CAPITAL
	8,300	500	2,000	2,000	8,300
6.	−1,200				−1,200
	7,100	500	2,000	2,000	7,600
	PROOF	9,600	=	PROOF	9,600

Summary: Incurred a business expense, decreasing owner's equity and the asset account Cash. The owner's equity changes because of business operations.

18

Transaction: Paid Office Max $1,200 on account.

> Mr. Jones has less cash in the bank following this transaction and his debts have decreased.

Transaction	Accounts Affected	Account Classification	Change in Balance
7. Paid Office Max $1,200 on account.	Accounts Payable	Liability	Decrease
	Cash	Asset	Decrease

	ASSETS			= LIABILITIES + CAPITAL	
TRANS NO.	CASH	SUPPLIES	EQUIPMENT	ACCOUNTS PAYABLE	CAPITAL
	7,100	500	2,000	2,000	7,600
7.	−1,200			−1,200	
	5,900	500	2,000	800	7,600
	PROOF	8,400	=	PROOF	8,400

Summary: The transaction reduced the value of the assets and at the same time reduced the debts of the business. The owner's equity remained the same.

Transaction: Paid Mang Association $700 for insurance.

> Insurance becomes an asset to a business because it is required to be prepaid in advance of its actual use. He has less cash in the bank following this transaction.

Transaction	Accounts Affected	Account Classification	Change in Balance
8. Paid Mang Association $700 for insurance.	Prepaid Insurance	Asset	Increase
	Cash	Asset	Decrease

	ASSETS				= LIABILITIES + CAPITAL	
TRANS NO.	CASH	SUPPLIES	EQUIPMENT	PREPAID INSURANCE	ACCOUNTS PAYABLE	CAPITAL
	5,900	500	2,000		2,000	7,600
8.	−700			+700		
	5,200	500	2,000	+700	800	7,600
			PROOF	8,400	= PROOF	8,400

Summary: The owner traded the value of one asset for another.

19

Transaction: Withdrew $600 for personal use.

When Mr. Jones withdraws cash for personal use, his equity decreases because he is using his own capital. A sole proprietor cannot be paid a salary; therefore, he must use his equity for his own personal living expenses. He has less cash in the bank following this transaction.

Transaction	Accounts Affected	Account Classification	Change in Balance
9. Withdrew $600 for personal use.	Capital	Capital	Decrease
	Cash	Asset	Decrease

ASSETS = LIABILITIES + CAPITAL

TRANS NO.	CASH	SUPPLIES	EQUIPMENT	PREPAID INSURANCE	ACCOUNTS PAYABLE	CAPITAL
	5,200	500	2,000		2,000	7,600
9.	−600					-600
	4,600	500	2,000	+700	800	7,000
			PROOF	7,800 =	PROOF	7,800

Summary: The owner's capital decreases anytime he/she draws money from the business for personal use. Also, the asset account Cash decreases. Note the accounting equation is still in balance.

Classify the following accounts by writing *A* for asset, *L* for liability or *C* for capital.

3.8 _____ Cash

3.9 _____ Drawing

3.10 _____ Prepaid Insurance

3.11 _____ Equipment

3.12 _____ Furniture Mart (for office furniture purchased on account)

3.13 _____ Supplies

3.14 _____ Second National Bank (for business loan)

SUMMARY OF TRANSACTIONS FOR JOE JONES, ACCOUNTANT

Transaction #	Accounts Affected	Account Classification	Change in Balance
1.	Cash	Asset	Increase
	Capital	Capital	Increase
2.	Supplies	Asset	Increase
	Cash	Asset	Decrease
3.	Equipment	Asset	Increase
	Accounts Payable	Liability	Increase
4.	Cash	Asset	Increase
	Capital	Capital	Increase
5.	Capital	Capital	Decrease
	Cash	Asset	Decrease
6.	Capital	Capital	Decrease
	Cash	Asset	Decrease
7.	Accounts Payable	Liability	Decrease
	Cash	Asset	Decrease
8.	Prepaid Insurance	Asset	Increase
	Cash	Asset	Decrease
9.	Capital	Capital	Decrease
	Cash	Asset	Decrease

	ASSETS				= LIABILITIES + CAPITAL	
TRANS NO.	CASH	SUPPLIES	EQUIPMENT	PREPAID INSURANCE	ACCOUNTS PAYABLE	CAPITAL
1.	6,000					+6,000
2.	− 500	+500				
Balance	5,500	500				6,000
3.			2,000		2,000	
Balance	5,500	500	2,000		2,000	6,000
4.	+3,500					+3,500
Balance	9,000	500	2,000		2,000	9,500
5.	− 700					−700
Balance	8,300	500	2,000		2,000	8,800
6.	−1,200					−1,200
Balance	7,100	500	2,000		2,000	7,600
7.	−1,200				−1,200	
Balance	5,900	500	2,000		800	7,600
8.	− 700			+700		
Balance	5,200	500	2,000	+700	800	7,600
9.	− 600					−600
Balance	4,600	500	2,000	700	800	7,000

BALANCE PROOF   Total of Assets: $7,800 = Liabilities + Capital: $7,800

Complete the following transactions.

Analyze each transaction to determine the following:

a. **Accounts Affected** – Cash, Supplies, Equipment, Prepaid Insurance, Accounts Payable, or Capital

b. **Account Classification** – asset, liability or capital

c. **Change in Balance** – increase or decrease

3.15

Transaction	Accounts Affected	Account Classification	Change in Balance
Owner invested $8,000 in the business.	a.		
	b.		

3.16

Transaction	Accounts Affected	Account Classification	Change in Balance
Received $1,500 in fees for the week.	a.		
	b.		

3.17

Transaction	Accounts Affected	Account Classification	Change in Balance
Paid rent for the month, $1,200.	a.		
	b.		

3.18

Transaction	Accounts Affected	Account Classification	Change in Balance
Paid salaries, $2,400.	a.		
	b.		

3.19

Transaction	Accounts Affected	Account Classification	Change in Balance
Bought supplies for $400 cash.	a.		
	b.		

ACCOUNTING

one

LIFEPAC TEST

107 / 134

LIFEPAC TEST ACCOUNTING 1

PART I

Circle the letter of the answer that best completes each statement (each answer, 1 point).

1. The purpose of accounting is to:

   a. provide accurate financial information   b. record transactions

   c. audit bills   d. manage business affairs

2. The person responsible for recording business transactions is the:

   a. accountant   b. receptionist

   c. bookkeeper   d. office manager

3. The first job at the bottom of the career ladder is called a/an:

   a. manager   b. entry-level job

   c. office manager   d. district manager

4. The task of planning, keeping, analyzing and interpreting business financial records is known as:

   a. bookkeeping   b. general office filing

   c. accounting   d. secretarial duties

5. The person assigned to plan, summarize, analyze and interpret a business's accounting records is a/an:

   a. accountant   b. office clerk

   c. bookkeeper   d. accounting clerk

6. An employee who does general kinds of office work, including some bookkeeping, is known as a/an:

   a. accountant   b. general office clerk

   c. accounting clerk   d. payroll clerk

7. An employee assigned to record, sort and file financial information is a/an:

   a. accountant   b. bookkeeper

   c. general office clerk   d. accounting clerk

8. The concept of preparing reports or financial records to cover a specific period of time is:

   a. business entity   b. objective evidence

   c. accounting period cycle   d. unit of measurement

9. Providing owners and managers with all financial information on statements they can easily interpret is:

   a. adequate disclosure
   b. accounting cycle
   c. objective evidence
   d. consistent reporting

10. Keeping the owner's personal assets and liabilities separated from the business assets and liabilities is the application of the concept of:

    a. adequate disclosure
    b. business entity
    c. objective evidence
    d. consistent reporting

11. Recording business transactions and preparing reports in such a way that they can be compared year after year is an application of the concept:

    a. adequate disclosure
    b. objective evidence
    c. consistent reporting
    d. accounting period cycle

12. Recording and summarizing accounting information are the primary job responsibilities of:

    a. an accounting clerk
    b. an accountant
    c. a general office clerk
    d. bookkeeper

13. Recording the value of an asset or liability at the actual price paid is the application of the concept of:

    a. historical costs
    b. objective evidence
    c. unit of measurement
    d. consistent reporting

14. Making sure that all expenses reported and all revenue earned are recorded in the same accounting period is known as:

    a. historical costs
    b. objective evidence
    c. matching expenses with revenue
    d. consistent reporting

15. Preparing a check stub or comparing a sales invoice with the purchase order is an example of:

    a. objective evidence
    b. consistent reporting
    c. unit of measurement
    d. historical costs

16. Recording a sales transaction when a sale is made instead of when the cash is received is applying the concept of:

    a. consistent reporting
    b. matching expenses with revenue
    c. realization of revenue
    d. objective evidence

17. Recording transactions and reporting financial information in dollars and cents is applying the concept of:

    a. unit of measurement
    b. consistent reporting
    c. historical costs
    d. adequate disclosure

18. A business owned by an individual who assumes all risks and operates with the purpose of making a profit is a:

    a. partnership
    b. corporation
    c. sole proprietorship
    d. cooperative

19. The owner of a business is known as the:

    a. president
    b. manager
    c. proprietor
    d. creditor

20. An association of two or more persons to carry out the functions of a business as co-owners is a:

    a. corporation
    b. partnership
    c. sole proprietorship
    d. cooperative

21. The most important disadvantage to consider when forming a sole proprietorship is:

    a. limited financial resources
    b. lack of continuity
    c. management problems
    d. unlimited liability

22. Most sole proprietorships fail because of:

    a. fraud
    b. lack of management skills
    c. neglect of the business
    d. lack of opportunities for employees

23. The most popular form of business ownership in the United States is:

    a. sole proprietorship
    b. partnership
    c. corporation
    d. cooperative

24. The business organization that produces the smallest dollar volume of business is a:

    a. corporation
    b. partnership
    c. sole proprietorship
    d. syndicate

25. Items that a business *owns* are known as:

    a. property
    b. equities
    c. liabilities
    d. assets

26. Accountants developed an equation to illustrate the relationship between assets, liabilities and capital. This equation is called:

a. financial mathematics

b. basic accounting equation

c. matching expenses with revenue

d. future value of assets

27. Any amount *owed* by a business is known as a/an:

a. asset

b. capital

c. equity

d. liability

28. All claims against the business are called:

a. liabilities

b. equities

c. assets

d. debts

29. The normal changes in the value of assets, liabilities and capital are brought about by:

a. business transactions

b. government regulation

c. equation change

d. business contract

30. The Basic Accounting Equation is represented by the total value of all:

a. assets and capital

b. assets, liabilities and capital

c. liabilities and capital

d. liabilities and assets

PART II

Complete the following exercise (104 points).

On June 1, Martha Smith opened a title searching business. The following transactions occurred during June:

1. Invested $6,000 cash in new business.

2. Rented an office, paying $1,500 cash.

3. Paid $180 for cleaning services.

4. Received $2,500 from a client for a title search.

5. Purchased office supplies on credit, $260.

6. Completed a title search for $1,500 on credit to be paid for at a later time.

7. Paid office salaries, $850 cash.

8. Paid $260 on account for supplies purchased earlier in the month.

9. Received payment of $1,500 on account.

10. Completed a title search for $1,100 on credit to be paid at a later date.

11. Bought office supplies on account, $350.

12. Received $1,100 cash for a title search completed previously.

13. Paid office salaries, $850 cash.

14. Paid the June telephone bill, $95.

15. Paid the June electric bill, $385.

16. Purchased liability insurance for the business, $2,400.

17. Withdrew $1,600 for personal use.

Instructions:

1. Enter the names of the following accounts on the top line of the accounting equation form on the next page: **Cash**; **Accounts Receivable**; **Prepaid Insurance**; **Office Supplies**; **Accounts Payable**; **Martha Smith, Capital**.

2. Show the effects of each transaction on the basic accounting equation by recording the increases (+) and decreases (−) in the proper column. Determine the correct balance after each transaction.

3. Check the balance at the end of the problem.

TRANS NO.						
1.						
2.						
Balance						
3.						
Balance						
4.						
Balance						
5.						
Balance						
6.						
Balance						
7.						
Balance						
8.						
Balance						
9.						
Balance						
10.						
Balance						
11.						
Balance						
12.						
Balance						
13.						
Balance						
14.						
Balance						
15.						
Balance						
16.						
Balance						
17.						
Balance						

BALANCE PROOF: Total of Assets: _____ = Liabilities + Capital: _____

NOTES

3.20

Transaction	Accounts Affected		Account Classification	Change in Balance
Bought insurance on account, $3,400.	a.			
	b.			

 Review the material in this section in preparation for the Self Test. This Self Test will check your mastery of this particular section as well as your knowledge of the previous sections.

SELF TEST 3

Match the following accounting terms with their definitions (each answer, 2 points).

3.01 _____ claims against assets

3.02 _____ items owned or controlled by a business

3.03 _____ the owner's equity in a business

3.04 _____ any amounts that are owed by a business

3.05 _____ a person responsible for recording business transactions

3.06 _____ an owner's withdrawal of cash from his business for personal use

3.07 _____ a formula that illustrates the relationship between assets, liabilities and capital

3.08 _____ an association of two or more persons to carry on as co-owners of a business for profit

3.09 _____ the dollar, for example

3.010 _____ a person responsible for analyzing business transactions

3.011 _____ activity that causes changes in the value of assets, liabilities and capital

3.012 _____ every business transaction is supported by a source document to prove the transaction occurred

3.013 _____ the period of time the books are open to record transactions and summarize account information

a. the accounting equation

b. partnership

c. equities

d. drawing

e. objective evidence

f. bookkeeper

g. assets

h. liabilities

i. unit of measurement

j. depreciation

k. business entity

l. accountant

m. business transaction

n. fiscal period

o. capital

Answer *true* **or** *false* (each answer, 2 points).

3.014 _____ The sole proprietorship is the most common form of business ownership in the United States.

3.015 _____ If necessary, accounting concepts are applied differently for each accounting period.

3.016 _____ One of the disadvantages of a sole proprietorship is the heavier burden of taxes and government regulation.

3.017 _____ Whenever a business owner withdraws money from the business for personal use, he is increasing the value of his capital account.

3.018 _____ In a sole proprietorship the owner's decisions are final.

3.019 _____ The accounting equation must always balance.

3.020 _____ Every business transaction changes at least three accounts in the accounting equation.

3.021 _____ Anytime a business pays out cash, the value of the cash account decreases.

3.022 _____ It is usually easier for a partnership to borrow funds because the responsibility of the debt is upon more than one person.

3.023 _____ Stockholders are personally liable for the debts of the corporation.

3.024 _____ If a business transaction increases one side of the accounting equation, then the other side must be decreased by the same amount.

Answer the following questions (each answer, 4 points).

3.025 What three questions must be asked when analyzing a business transaction?

a. _____

b. _____

c. _____

3.026 What are three things that can cause decreases to the assets of a business?

a. _____

b. _____

c. _____

SECTION IV. REVIEW & APPLICATION PROBLEMS

Summary

1. The nature of accounting is to provide accurate financial information needed by business owners, managers, creditors and governmental agencies.

2. Accountants and bookkeepers are responsible for providing this data.

3. Many career opportunities are available for persons interested in working with business finances.

4. The accounting profession is guided by basic accounting concepts.

5. The three most common forms of business ownership are: sole proprietorships, partnerships and corporations.

6. The most common form of business in the United States is the sole proprietorship.

7. The advantages of a sole proprietorship are: ownership of all profits, owner is boss, tax savings, secrecy and ease of organization and dissolution.

8. The disadvantages of a sole proprietorship are: unlimited liability, limited resources, management problems and lack of continuity.

9. The type and size of the business usually determine how accounting records are kept: either manually, with accounting machines, or with computerized accounting systems.

10. Assets are items owned by a business entity in order to produce future benefits.

11. Liabilities are debts owed to others.

12. Capital is the owner's net worth after settling all debts.

13. The relationship between assets, liabilities and capital is expressed by the basic accounting equation: Assets = Liabilities + Capital.

14. Given two elements of the accounting equation, the equation can be arranged mathematically to determine the missing element.

15. Investments by the owner increase capital while withdrawals decrease the owner's capital.

16. Revenues received from services preformed or items sold increase equity while expenses of business operation decrease equity.

17. All changes are recorded in a business transaction.

18. Each transaction requires the following analysis: accounts affected, classification of the affected accounts and how the balances are changed.

19. Every business transaction changes at least two accounts in the accounting equation.

20. If the changes occur only on one side of the equation, all increases on that side must be matched with decreases on the same side.

21. If the transaction increases one side of the equation, then the other side must be increased by the same amount.

22. If the transaction decreases one side of the equation, then the other side must be decreased by the same amount.

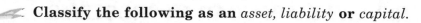 **Classify the following as an** *asset, liability* **or** *capital.*

4.1

ACCOUNT	CLASSIFICATION
a. Cash	
b. Accounts Payable	
c. Land	
d. Supplies	
e. Notes Payable	
f. Equipment	
g. Owner's Investment	
h. Any amount owed	
i. Anything owned	
j. Joe Jones, Capital	
k. Prepaid Insurance	

Identify the changes made to capital by the following transactions. Indicate whether the change will cause an *increase,* **a** *decrease* **or** *no change.*

4.2

TRANSACTIONS	CHANGE TO CAPITAL
a. Bought supplies on account	
b. Paid cash for monthly rent	
c. Paid the amount owed for supplies	
d. Received fees for services rendered	
e. Bought business insurance	
f. Additional investment by owner	
g. Paid the monthly utility bill	

26

Identify changes to the accounting equation caused by the following business transactions. Read each transaction carefully and in the columns below indicate the NET EFFECT made to the TOTAL VALUE of assets, liabilities and capital. Write *increase*, *decrease* or *no effect*. The first transaction is done for you as an example.

Transactions:

1. Owner invested cash in a business.
2. Purchased supplies for cash.
3. Received fees for services rendered.
4. Purchased equipment on account.
5. Paid the salaries for the week.
6. Paid the balance owed for equipment bought on account.
7. Withdrew cash for personal use.

		TRANS. NO.	ASSETS	=	LIABILITIES	+	CAPITAL
4.3	a.	1.	*increase*		*no effect*		*increase*
	b.	2.					
	c.	3.					
	d.	4.					
	e.	5.					
	f.	6.					
	g.	7.					

Analyze each of the following transactions to determine which items in the accounting equation are affected. Accounts include: Cash, Supplies, Equipment, Accounts Payable and Capital.

Transactions for Green's Dentistry:

1. Invested $9,600 in cash to begin operations.
2. Purchased dental equipment for $2,400 cash.
3. Paid $900 cash for rent on the office space for this month.
4. Purchased additional equipment on account, $6,600.
5. Received $1,500 for services rendered.
6. Received $2,700 for services rendered.
7. Purchased supplies for $480 cash.
8. Paid wages to dental assistant, $1,200.
9. Paid for dental equipment previously bought on account, $6,600.
10. Paid cash for the utility bill for the month, $1,100.

4.4

Transaction No.	Accounts Affected	Account Classification	Change in Balance
1.			
2.			
3.			
4.			
5.			
6.			
7.			
8.			
9.			
10.			

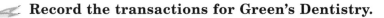

Record the transactions for Green's Dentistry.

Instructions:

a. Using the transaction information on the previous page, write the amount in the proper column, using a (+) to indicate an increase in the value of any account and a (−) to indicate a decrease in the value of any account.

b. After each entry, record the new balance.

c. Check that the accounting equation is in balance before recording the next transaction. The first transaction has been done for you as an example.

	ASSETS			= LIABILITIES + CAPITAL	
TRANS NO.	CASH	SUPPLIES	EQUIPMENT	ACCOUNTS PAYABLE	CAPITAL
1.	+9,600				+9,600
2.					
Balance					
3.					
Balance					
4.					
Balance					
5.					
Balance					
6.					
Balance					
7.					
Balance					
8.					
Balance					
9.					
Balance					
10.					
Balance					

4.5

BALANCE PROOF: Total of Assets: _____ = Liabilities + Capital: _____

 Analyze each transaction to determine which items on the accounting equation are affected.

James King operates a janitorial service called **Clean-Rite**. This is a professional cleaning service used by other businesses. The transactions below are those completed by his business during one week. Use the form on the next page to analyze the transactions for this business. The accounts Mr. King uses include: Cash, Supplies, Prepaid Insurance, Accounts Payable and J. King, Capital.

Transactions for Clean-Rite:

1. Paid cash for month's rent, $700
2. Received cash from daily sales, $600.
3. Received cash from the owner as an additional investment, $2,000.
4. Paid cash for repairs to cleaning equipment, $25.
5. Paid cash on account, $150.
6. Received cash from daily sales, $800.
7. Paid the water bill, $45.
8. Paid cash for insurance, $200.
9. Paid cash for supplies, $100.
10. Received cash from daily sales, $500.
11. Paid cash to owner for personal use, $200.
12. Paid cash for the telephone bill, $100.
13. Paid cash on account, $350.
14. Received cash from daily sales, $700.
15. Paid cash for a classified ad, $25.
16. Received cash from daily sales, $150.

4.6

Transaction No.	Accounts Affected	Account Classification	Change in Balance
1.			
2.			
3.			
4.			
5.			
6.			
7.			
8.			
9.			
10.			
11.			
12.			
13.			
14.			
15.			
16.			

Determine how a transaction changes an accounting equation.

Instructions:

a. **Enter the names of the accounts** for Clean-Rite on the top line of the accounting equation sheet on the next page.
   Assets: **Cash**, **Supplies**, **Prepaid Insurance**
   Liabilities: **Accounts Payable**
   Capital: **J. King, Capital**

b. **Write the amount in the proper column**, using a (+) to indicate an increase in the value of any account and a (−) to indicate a decrease in the value of any account.

c. **Record the new balance** after each entry.

d. **Check** that the accounting equation is in balance before recording the next transaction.

Transactions for Clean-Rite:

1. Record the following balances for the accounts: **Cash**, $1500; **Supplies**, $1800; **Prepaid Insurance**, $300; **Accounts Payable**, $850; **Capital**, $2,750.
2. Paid cash for month's rent, $700.
3. Received cash from daily sales, $600.
4. Received cash from the owner as an additional investment, $2,000.
5. Paid cash for repairs to cleaning equipment, $25.
6. Paid cash on account, $150.
7. Received cash from daily sales, $800.
8. Paid cash for the water bill, $45.
9. Paid cash for insurance, $200.
10. Paid cash for supplies, $100.
11. Received cash from daily sales, $500.
12. Paid cash to owner for personal use, $200.
13. Paid cash for the telephone bill, $100.
14. Paid cash on account, $350.
15. Received cash from daily sales, $700.
16. Paid cash for a classified ad, $25.
17. Received cash from daily sales, $150.

	ASSETS			= LIABILITIES + CAPITAL	
TRANS NO.					
1.					
2.					
Balance					
3.					
Balance					
4.					
Balance					
5.					
Balance					
6.					
Balance					
7.					
Balance					
8.					
Balance					
9.					
Balance					
10.					
Balance					
11.					
Balance					
12.					
Balance					
13.					
Balance					
14.					
Balance					
15.					
Balance					
16.					
Balance					
17.					
Balance					

4.7

BALANCE PROOF: Total of Assets: _____ = Liabilities + Capital: _____

Determine how transactions change an accounting equation.

Henry Harrison operates a surveying service called **Map-It**. Henry is a licensed surveyor and his services are used by a number of real estate agents. He began his business with the assets listed below. The transactions listed below were completed by his business during one week.

Instructions:

a. **Enter the names of the accounts** on the top line of the accounting equation sheet.
   Assets: **Cash, Supplies, Prepaid Insurance** and **Equipment**
   Liabilities: **Accounts Payable**
   Capital: **H. Harrison, Capital**

b. **Analyze each transaction** to determine which items on the accounting equation are affected. In this problem you are not required to write out the analysis of each transaction, but you should review these concepts: (1) identify what accounts are affected, (2) classify the affected accounts (asset, liability, capital), and (3) determine how the account balances are affected (increase, decrease).

c. **Write the amount in the proper column**, using a (+) to indicate an increase in the value of any account and a (–) to indicate a decrease in the value of any account.

d. **Record the new balance** after each entry.

e. **Check** that the accounting equation is in balance before recording the next transaction.

Transactions for Map-It:

1. Record the following balance for the accounts: **Cash**, $2,500; **Supplies**, $1,150; **Prepaid Insurance**, $1,800; **Equipment**, $2,400; **Accounts Payable**, $1,850; **Capital**, $6,000
2. Paid cash for month's rent, $900.
3. Received cash from surveying fees, $950.
4. Received cash from the owner as an additional investment, $1,800.
5. Paid cash for repairs to surveying equipment, $25.
6. Paid cash on account, $1,150.
7. Received cash from surveying fees, $800.
8. Paid the telephone bill, $65.
9. Paid cash for insurance, $800.
10. Paid cash for surveying supplies, $600.
11. Received cash from surveying fees, $750.
12. Paid cash to owner for personal use, $1,200.
13. Paid cash for the electric bill, $400.
14. Purchased surveying supplies on account, $850. (This creates an additional value to Accounts Payable.)
15. Received cash from surveying fees, $700.
16. Paid cash for a classified ad, $225.
17. Received cash from surveying fees, $250.

	ASSETS			= LIABILITIES + CAPITAL		
TRANS NO.						
1.						
2.						
Balance						
3.						
Balance						
4.						
Balance						
5.						
Balance						
6.						
Balance						
7.						
Balance						
8.						
Balance						
9.						
Balance						
10.						
Balance						
11.						
Balance						
12.						
Balance						
13.						
Balance						
14.						
Balance						
15.						
Balance						
16.						
Balance						
17.						
Balance						

4.8

BALANCE PROOF: Total of Assets: _____ = Liabilities + Capital: _____

Determine how transactions change an accounting equation.

John Oats, CPA, began an accounting practice last month. His business uses the following accounts:

      Assets: **Cash, Accounts Receivable, Office Supplies, Office Equipment and Building**

      Liabilities: **Accounts Payable, Notes Payable**

      Capital: **John Oats, Capital**

Instructions:

a.   **Enter the names of the accounts** on the top line of the accounting equation sheet.

Mr. Oats created a new asset account called **Accounts Receivable**. This account is used when a client wishes to charge the services rendered. The account is increased for every charge, along with the owner's capital account. The account is decreased when payment is received and the Cash account is increased. However, the increase to cash is not recorded until the money is actually paid. Normally, an account ending with the word "Receivable" is an asset, because the balance of this account represents money to be collected by the business. In effect, the business owns the right to collect the money due. Other examples of receivables are: Notes Receivable, Subscriptions Receivable, Dues Receivable and Contributions Receivable.

Mr. Oats also has a new liability account called **Notes Payable**. This account is used when he borrows money to operate his business. When Mr. Oats pays an installment payment on Notes Payable, the account is decreased because he owes less money and the Cash account is decreased because he is paying out cash. Normally, an account ending with the word "Payable" is a liability, because the balance of the account represents money to be paid by the business. Legally, the business has created a promise to pay money to another business or person. Other examples of payables are: Federal Income Taxes Payable, Mortgage Payable and Sales Tax Payable.

b.   **Analyze each transaction on the next page** to determine which items in the accounting equation are affected.

c.   **Write the amount in the proper column**, using a (+) to indicate an increase in the value of any account and a (–) to indicate a decrease in the value of any account.

d.   **Record the new balance** after each entry.

e.   **Check** that the accounting equation is in balance before recording the next transaction.

Transactions for John Oats, CPA:

1. Sold for $53,700 a personal investment in IBM stock and deposited $50,000 of the proceeds in a bank account in the name of the accounting practice.
2. Purchased for $150,000 a small office building to be used for his practice. He paid $45,000 in cash and signed a note payable promising to pay the balance over a period of 10 years.
3. Took office equipment from home for use in the accounting practice. The equipment had a value of $500.
4. Purchased office supplies for cash, $550.
5. Purchased office equipment on credit, $7,500.
6. Received $630 cash from a client after completing the monthly accounting work.
7. Paid $250 cash for a newspaper advertisement for the accounting practice.
8. Completed $1,900 of accounting work for a firm on credit. The firm wished to be billed at a later date.
9. Made a $750 installment payment on the equipment purchased on account.
10. Received on account $1,900 from a client. (This is the client we permitted to charge earlier in the month.)
11. Paid $650 cash to the office secretary for wages.
12. John Oats withdrew $450 from the bank account for personal use.
13. Paid $2,000 cash installment on the notes payable for the building.

	ASSETS				=	LIABILITIES + CAPITAL		
TRANS NO.								
1.								
2.								
Balance								
3.								
Balance								
4.								
Balance								
5.								
Balance								
6.								
Balance								
7.								
Balance								
8.								
Balance								
9.								
Balance								
10.								
Balance								
11.								
Balance								
12.								
Balance								
13.								
Balance								

BALANCE PROOF: Total of Assets: _____ = Liabilities + Capital: _____

Review the material in this section in preparation for the Self Test. This Self Test will check your mastery of this particular section as well as your knowledge of the previous sections.

SELF TEST 4

4.01 **Classify each of the following accounts as either an** *asset*, *liability* **or** *capital* (each answer, 1 point).

ACCOUNT	CLASSIFICATION
a. Cash	
b. Accounts Payable	
c. Automobile	
d. Notes Payable	
e. Accounts Receivable	
f. Mortgage Payable	
g. Owner's investment	
h. Any amount owed	
i. Anything owned	
j. Mary Smith, Capital	
k. Prepaid Insurance	
l. Sales Tax Payable	
m. Dues Receivable	
n. Federal Income Tax Payable	
o. Owner's Equity	

4.02 **Using the three elements of the accounting equation, determine the missing amount in each equation below** (each answer, 1 point).

	Assets	=	Liabilities	+	Capital
a.	$18,000	=	$12,000	+	_____
b.	$28,000	=	_____	+	$14,000
c.	_____	=	$22,000	+	$46,000
d.	$6,000	=	$3,200	+	_____
e.	$27,000	=	_____	+	$1,900
f.	_____	=	$2,300	+	$2,300

39

4.03   **Jane's Nails**, a new business owned by Jane Osgood, uses the following accounts: **Cash, Supplies, Prepaid Insurance, Accounts Payable and Jane Osgood, Capital.**

Instructions:

a. **Analyze each transaction** below to determine which items in the accounting equation are affected.

b. **Label the columns** on the accounting equation form on the next page, using the account titles listed above and record the transactions, making sure to use a (+) to indicate an increase in the value of any account and a (−) to indicate a decrease in the value of any account.

c. **Record the new balance** after each entry and **check that the accounting equation is in balance** before recording the next transaction.

d. **Enter the final balance proof.**

Transactions for Jane's Nails:

1. Owner invested cash, $3,500.
2. Bought supplies for cash, $600.
3. Paid cash for insurance, $550.
4. Bought supplies on account, $1,100.
5. Paid $350 on account.
6. Jane withdrew $100 for personal use.

Transaction Analysis for Jane's Nails (each answer, 1 point)

Transaction #	Accounts Affected	Account Classification	Change in Balance
1.			
2.			
3.			
4.			
5.			
6.			

Accounting Equation Form (each answer, 1 point)

	ASSETS		= LIABILITIES + CAPITAL	

TRANS NO.					
1.					
2.					
Balance					
3.					
Balance					
4.					
Balance					
5.					
Balance					
6.					
Balance					

BALANCE PROOF: Total of Assets: _____ = Liabilities + Capital: _____

Score _____

Adult Check _____
Initial   Date

41

OPTIONAL EXERCISES FOR EXTRA CREDIT

Answer these questions (each answer, 3 points).

1. When you separate an owner's personal records from his business records, you are applying which business concept?

2. There are two types of equities in every business. What are they?

3. What does the accounting equation represent?

4. If a business purchases something on account, the business creates a _____.

5. What accounts are affected, and how, when the owner invests in a business?

6. How are liabilities changed when a business pays part of debt owed?

7. What is the basic accounting equation when written out as a mathematical equation?

8. What accounts are affected when the business receives income for services rendered?

9. What is the unit of measurement for business transactions?

10. What three questions should be asked when analyzing transactions?

Complete the following activity
(40 points).

George Smith began a law practice on July 1. Listed below are the accounts for his business.

Instructions:

a. **Arrange the following accounts** into assets, liabilities and capital: **Cash; Accounts Receivable; Office Supplies; Law Books; Office Equipment; Accounts Payable; and George Smith, Capital**.

b. **Label the columns** on the accounting equation form on the next page, using the account titles listed above.

c. **Record the transactions**, making sure to use a (+) to indicate an increase in the value of any account and a (−) to indicate a decrease in the value of any account.

d. **Record the new balance** after each entry and **check that the accounting equation is in balance** before recording the next transaction.

e. **Enter the final balance proof.**

Transactions for George Smith, Attorney at Law:

1. Invested $5,000 in cash and $9,500 in office equipment in the practice.
2. Rented an office for $600 cash.
3. Purchased legal reference books for cash, $900.
4. Purchased office supplies for cash, $110.
5. Purchased additional reference books costing $2,500. Paid $1,000 in cash and promised to pay the balance in 90 days.
6. Received $670 in legal fees.
7. Purchased office supplies on account, $560.
8. Completed a will for a client for $150. The client charged the fee to be paid at a later time.
9. Received $150 on account for will completed earlier.
10. Received $1,500 in legal fees.
11. Paid $300 on account for supplies charged earlier.
12. Paid the telephone bill, $70 cash.
13. Mr. Smith took $1,400 for personal use from the business funds.

TRANS NO.							
1.							
2.							
Balance							
3.							
Balance							
4.							
Balance							
5.							
Balance							
6.							
Balance							
7.							
Balance							
8.							
Balance							
9.							
Balance							
10.							
Balance							
11.							
Balance							
12.							
Balance							
13.							
Balance							

BALANCE PROOF: Total of Assets: _____ = Liabilities + Capital: _____